Zdeněk Pavliš

Hockey
The Basics

Meyer & Meyer Sport

Original Title: Abeceda Hokejového Bruslení
© Zdeněk Pavliš, 1996
Translated from the German by James Beachus

British Library Cataloguing in Publication Data
A catalogue record for this book is available from the British Library

Pavlis, Zdenek:
Hockey – The Basics
Oxford: Meyer & Meyer Sport (UK) Ltd., 2003
ISBN 1-84126-128-9

© 2003 by Meyer & Meyer Sport (UK) Ltd.
Aachen, Adelaide, Auckland, Budapest, Graz, Johannesburg,
Miami, Olten (CH), Oxford, Singapore, Toronto
Member of the World
Sports Publishers' Association (WSPA)
www.w-s-p-a.org
Coverphoto: getty images, Munich
Printed and bound by: FINIDR, s. r. o., Český Těšín
ISBN 1-84126-128-9
E-Mail: verlag@m-m-sports.com
www.m-m-sports.com

CONTENTS

have tried to bring together in this book all the known theoretical and practical knowledge from ice hockey. In addition, I have included practical experience that I have gained, bit by bit, from many long years of training work, and which I have tested myself.

I have gone into a description of the basic skating techniques from a technical and methodical point of view and this includes a description of the individual learning steps. The text has been complemented by numerous diagrams and picture series. These should serve to be of use for those, who are starting to train children for the first time and do not possess much practical experience.

The individual ice-skating techniques have been laid out such that their description corresponds with a well-tried complete system. On the face of it, it appears that the layout is seemingly comprehensive, however, if the reader looks closer it soon becomes clear that only the basic movements and skills necessary for correct ice-skating are covered. There are also descriptions of the most common mistakes.

For use in exercises, there are 25 little games to practice movements on the ice and 45 skating exercises that serve to improve ice-skating skills. The exercises in the book present a suggestion for training and the trainer can use them to create other variations.

It is quite clear that this book cannot provide a totally complete overview of all the knowledge and experience of skating in ice hockey. Nevertheless, I have tried to select the most important aspects of the theme. Whether this has succeeded or not is up to the reader. In any case, I would be grateful for comments or suggestions.

Zdeněk Pavliš

SKATING IN HOCKEY

A s the fastest team sport, ice hockey is very much characterized by the requirement for correct skating. Skating in ice hockey is the most difficult skill and demands relatively long periods of practise. There are many parameters in mastering it. To be an excellent player, he must possess all the ice-skating skills.

Perfect ice-skating is the essential starting point for the player in all technical and tactical skills. If the player has to accomplish different playing skills (shooting, defending etc.) at high speed, and at the same time control play, then it is extremely important that he can do all these things without having to concentrate on skating. Thus, ice-skating is the cornerstone upon which all the other stones – ice hockey skills - can be built.

Children, who want to play as young ice hockey players, should begin ice-skating at the age of 5-6, and in the first two years 80% of the training time should be spent ice-skating.

For effective ice-skating training with children, a practical demonstration is absolutely necessary. If the trainer is not able to do this himself perfectly, he should get an active player to give the demonstration. In addition to the visual element of the demonstration, it is also a necessity as the young players will be able to copy the grown-ups.

The space where the young player practices ice-skating is important. On a small playing area he has to use the cross-over often and change direction. On the other hand, a large area offers good conditions for gliding.

The next factor also plays an important role in the ice-skating technique. Here it is to do with the quality of the ice surface. One hears of opinions in training circles that young icehockey players do not need perfect ice conditions. However, practice shows quite clearly that a well-prepared ice surface belongs to the most important requirements for successful ice-skating training.

9

Requirements for Successful Training in Ice-skating

- Training should take place three times a week - in a period of 60 minutes each - excepting the general preparation off the ice rink.
- For the training, a well-prepared ice surface must be available.
- Assistants should take part in the training. This allows the team to be split up into small groups (ideally 5-6 players per group).
- Exercises in the form of play are preferred as a training routine.
- For ice-skating training it is not necessary to wear all the ice hockey equipment. For the beginner it is sufficient to wear the helmet complete with face protector, gloves (not necessarily those specially made for ice hockey), the elbow and shin protector pads, the correct length ice hockey stick (this reaches up to the chin for a player standing on ice-skates, see Diagram 1).

Diagram 1

- For the correct ice-skating technique, attention must be given to the selection of the skates. Above all they must be the correct size and quality. The optimum skate is large enough so that there is room for socks in them. The best skates are those with conventional lacing and built-in ankle protection. The runners must of course be honed.
- The exercising of all the skills must be carried out, allowing the same amount of time for each of them. All exercises must be carried out with **each** leg (e.g., the cross-over to the left and to the right) and in **both** directions (skating backwards as often as skating forwards). Every person, however, manages each exercise better on one side than the other (usually it is the left side). Because of this, training begins with the side that the player finds easiest (e.g., the cross-over to the left). Later on, the more difficult side is exercised more often than initially.
- First of all, the basics of ice-skating are exercised without a stick and with a stiff upper-body. The fixed upper-body allows the player, later on, to separate the movements of the hands (dribbling the puck or shooting) from those of the feet. Therefore a start position of standing with the arms stretched out to the sides is recommended. The arms are still a little under the height of the shoulders and held slightly forward, so that the player can see both thumbs in his field of vision. Another recommended position to keep the arms fixed is holding them behind the back with the hands grasping the elbows.
- After mastering all the basics of ice-skating it is also necessary to practice all possible exercises with the stick.
- According to each person's capabilities, the players are divided up into small groups. Each group then follows a different training program.
- A perfect demonstration is combined with a comprehensible explanation from the trainer dependent on the age of the class.
- Further methods have also been proved in practical sessions. Nevertheless, they don't stay the same for ever. Dependent on the ability of the ice-skaters, it is quite possible, and sometimes even advisable, to begin with some exercises earlier or leave them out, bringing them in later. Some skills can also be exercised at the same time. Each trainer must be able to judge this for himself and select the correct sequence, so that the training can run effectively and without any problems.
- Long years of experience show that for the training of basic skills, figure skating lends itself to this.

Recommended Sequence for the Training of Individual Ice-Skating Skills

- Ice-skating forwards
- Braking when skating forwards
- Skating in a curve and doing the cross-over forwards
- Skating backwards
- Braking when skating backwards
- Doing the cross-over backwards
- Turns
- Starts
- Skating skills and Tricks

For systematic reasons, the individual ice-skating skills in this book have been laid out differently. In practice, however, the recommended sequence has proved to work well.

2 SKATING FORWARDS

Before we can move on to the actual techniques and methods of the skills in ice-skating, first of all, the correct basic stance has to be explained. The legs are bent at the hips, knees and ankles. The angle at the knee-joints is between 90° and 120°. The head is held up and the player looks forward at a spot on the ground about 30m away. The stick is held in both hands (see Diagrams 2a and 2b). There are two variations of the basic stance – one is in a higher standing position and the other is lower. In the lower stance the legs are bent more, which gives the best condition for a powerful push-off. In this stance the leg muscles tire quickly. The weight of the body is centered more forwards. The basic stance must be individually adopted so that the body doesn't cramp up, but remains relaxed.

Diagrams 2a and 2b

Correct Technique

Skating forwards out of the basic stance already described is one of the basic movements of every ice hockey player. It is a cyclic movement made up of the following phases:

- **Adopt the position**
- **Push-off and glide** (forwards and sideways)
- **Changeover legs**

When **adopting the starting position** with the skates it is important that both legs are in the so-called **"T-position"** (heels behind each other) – see Diagrams 3a and 3b.

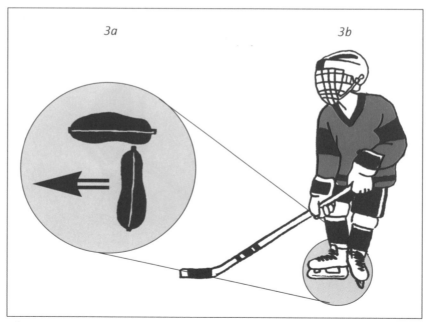

Diagrams 3a and 3b

The skate is first of all placed on the ice on the outer-edge of the runner and then turned over onto the inside-edge of the runner (the movement resembles a long extended "S" shape). Placing the skate down starts with the tip of the foot and ends the same way (see Diagrams 4a and 4b)

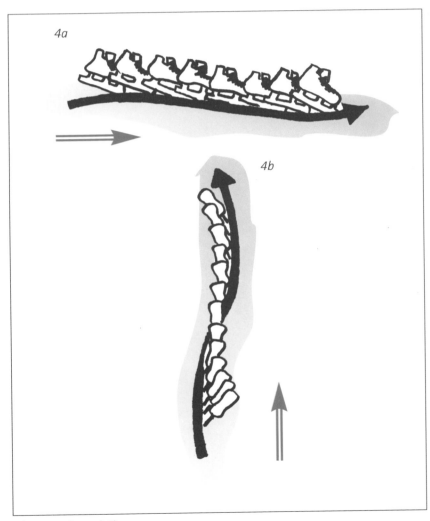

Diagrams 4a and 4b

The **push-off**, which has a considerable influence over the speed of ice-skating, is carried out on the whole of the inside-edge of the runner – slanting backwards and to the side - by powerfully tensing the leg at the knee and hip joints. It is important that the leg is quite bent (at an angle of between 90° and 120° – see Diagram 5).

Diagram 5

The knee of the bent leg should reach forward beyond the tip of the foot (see Diagram 6).

Diagram 6

In this way a dynamic push-off can be achieved while at the same time giving a good sense and feeling in mastering the skates. It is not correct to lift the leg up too high above the ice after the push-off. If this happens, the movement then becomes uneconomic and prevents a correct setting down of the skate again. When changing over legs the leg is bent but the muscles remain relaxed. At the moment that the other leg finishes the push-off, with the skate still on the inside-edge, the initial leg sets the skate down on the ice on its outside-edge. One mistake is to take too long a stride.

A summary of the skating-step movements in the push-off with the left leg looks like this:

From the basic stance position the push-off is carried out from the whole length of the inside-edge of the runner. The weight of the body is transferred gradually onto the right leg as it picks up the gliding motion. After the push-off, the leg is lifted off the ice. At the moment that it is lifted off the ice it is stretched out almost to its full extent. The left leg is held just above the surface of the ice after the push-off and comes back into a position behind the right leg. Both legs are quite close together and are bent, and then the push-off with the right leg is carried out. The player lifts his head up, thus achieving a suitable torso position and an optimum condition for an efficient push-off. An important thing is to keep the body relaxed as the movements are made and that the accompanying hip motion is used to the best. The swinging of the arms at shoulder breadth also makes for a fluid skating movement (see Picture Series 1).

Picture Series 1

Skating forwards – the most important points

Basic Position

- Bent knee
- Body leaning forward slightly
- Head lifted up
- Stick held in both hands

Cycle: Push-off - Gliding - Push-off

- Turn the edge of the skate outwards
- Energetic push-off forwards on the inside edge
- End the push-off on the tip of the toe
- Transfer the body weight onto the push-off leg
- Moderate length of each step

Tips on Methods/Main Emphasis in Training

In order to get to grips with the basics of skating forwards it is very important, first of all, to gain a feeling of good balance and stability on the skates.

Sometimes, it is recommended to practice a few exercises off the ice rink before taking the first steps on the ice. This concerns exercises where the children are wearing their skates already. They can learn to walk, maintain their balance (on one leg as well as two), bend their knees and turn the tip of the foot outwards etc. After this they can practice on the ice. The following methods are recommended:

- One important skill, which the children must learn, is being able **to stand up again after a fall** - something that happens quite often, understandably, at the beginning. The player usually ends up in a sitting position or on his back or tummy. The aim is to stand up again from the lying position using the knees. If standing up is done with the help of the stick it should always be held in both hands (see Diagram 7).

Diagram 7

- Next come **balancing exercises on the spot**. Here they do standing on one leg, transferring the weight from one leg to the other, the knees-bend and standing up again, hopping etc. (see Diagram 8).

Diagram 8

Going slowly on the ice with a push-off to the side and forwards (wobbly steps). Good exercises to achieve this are walking holding onto the side barrier of the rink, being helped by a partner, going over obstacles, walking lifting up the knee high, bending to the side etc. It is very important to continually check that a correct starting position is being used, i.e., "one heel behind the other" (see Diagram 9).

Diagram 9

• **Gliding on both legs** is done by pushing off from the rink side barrier using both hands (see Diagram 10). The aim of the exercise is to glide as far as possible.

Diagram 10

- After managing the earlier exercises it is recommended to practice **transferring the body weight** from one leg to the other. This is followed up by doing knee-bends and gentle hopping.
- Gliding on one leg is done along the same lines as previously explained for gliding on both legs. After pushing off, it is a question of seeing how far one can glide. First of all, it's preferable to glide in a straight line and then to change over to gliding in an inside curve and then an outside curve. A good exercise for this is to imitate a "stork" (the leg is bent and held out to the front with the foot pulled back as far as the knee of the standing leg), or you can imitate an "automobile" (do a knees-bend with one leg stretched out forwards and stretch the arms out to the front) and so on. As a last phase you do gliding with your knees bent, bending up and down, trotting and other variations (see Diagram 11).

Diagram 11

- Now it's time to practice the **push-off and gliding** once you have mastered the balancing exercises. The basic exercise consists of doing a snake shape. A **double snake shape** is also called a "fish". This is done by alternately pushing the legs out (splits) and drawing them back in. You can see how the tracks look like in Diagram 12.

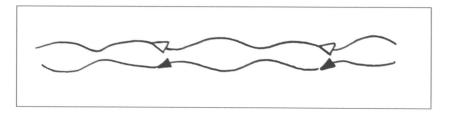

Diagram 12

The exercise is made considerably easier if the toe is turned outwards and the knees slightly bent when doing the splits (when drawing the legs back in - the opposite) (see Diagram 13).

Diagram 13

However, the exercise should be done by bending and stretching the knees and not always by strenuous splits and drawing the legs together. Before doing the first exercises, foot movements standing on the spot should be done - outwards and in-wards. In this way you avoid a certain amount of risk of injury. While children can push their legs apart without a problem, getting them back together is more diffi-cult. A parallel, double snake shape is the next exercise (see Diagram 14).

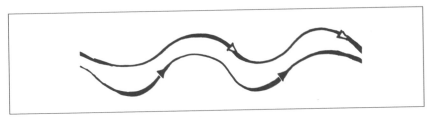

Diagram 14

Here you push-off with both legs alternately right and left. Each push-off occurs on the other edge (so-called wedel - like in skiing). Both legs, nevertheless, stay al-ways on the ice. It's preferable to get the knees to do the work (the push-off is not done as an energetic movement, rather by transferring the weight of the body over the corresponding leg).

Following on from this you can start doing the **snake shape on one leg**. There are three variations of this:

- Curve on the inside edge
- Curve on the outside edge
- Snake shape on one leg, changing the edges

For doing the exercises with the double and single curves, the following games and competitions are ideal for helping the children:

- Who can glide farthest on the right (left) leg?
- Relay race using the snake shape.
- All joining together as a snake and doing the snake shape.
- Who can skate the farthest with the minimum number of snake shapes etc.?

After doing these exercises we now turn to the actual push-off and gliding. There are a number of exercises for this also. The most popular are:

- Excercises at the barrier on the edge of the ice rink - this trains one to put the skate down on the ice correctly; the starting position is with the one heel behind the other (see Diagram 15).
- Exercises using a chair - see Diagram 16.
- Exercises with a partner - pushing, pulling (see Diagram 17).
- Various forms of skills and tricks (see Diagram 18).

Diagram 15

Diagram 16

Diagram 17

Diagram 18

Training for a skating rhythm was, up until now, one of the seemingly underestimated themes in ice hockey. Yet, the correct feeling for a skating rhythm has a bearing on the quality of ice-skating, mainly in skating forwards, backwards and when doing the cross-over. An incorrect rhythm can be detected in the absence of a smooth, continued flow of the skating movement ("limping"). training, various rhythmic exercises are recommended (for example skating to music and hopping at certain points etc.). The length of the skating step and the speed should be slightly increased, but only gradually.

The Main Mistakes in Technique

- Too much movement of the hips in an upright position (so-called "pumping"), which places the power in the up and down movement of the body rather than in the push-off.
- The push-off occurs from the tip of the skate rather than from the whole length of the runner.
- The push-off is done to the rear and is not aligned to be done as a side movement (the feet are lifted up behind the body) and as a result it is inefficient.
- The push-off is not done from the basic position (one heel behind the other) and too large a step is taken, which leads to a short push-off.
- The knees are only bent a little and the trunk of the body is too stiff.
- The skate is not set down on the ice parallel with the other skate, which is gliding.
- Incorrect rhythmic movement ("limping") which can come from an uneven push-off. The legs are being used with different emphasis and the skating steps are different lengths.
- When in the starting position the skate is lying on the surface of the ice rather than being just above it. With children, this often leads to tripping over the tip of the skate on the ice.
- The head is bent too far forward and you lose balance and direction.
- The upper body is bent too far to the rear so that the weight is transferred on to the heels.

3 SKATING BACKWARDS

Correct Technique

Ice-skating backwards is the second skill to be learned. In ice hockey today, it is extremely important that this technique is fully mastered by not only the forwards and strikers but also defenders. A good player can skate backwards just as well as forwards and almost just as fast.

In the basic position the legs are placed at the width of the hips, the head is held upright and the pelvis is tipped forward. The player holds the stick in one hand in front of the body. The weight of the body is distributed evenly on both legs (the skate runners are placed down on the ice on their whole length - see Diagram 19).

Diagram 19

The actual movement comes from the hip joint. From here it is transferred down to the tips of the feet. The shoulders are also used in the movement. The push-off is done from the inside edge of the skate each time (alternately right and left leg - see Diagram 20). It is done by repeatedly bending and tensing the knee-joint of the leg as you push the corresponding shoulder backwards and activate the hip-joint (see Diagram 21).

Diagram 20

Diagram 21

The push-off starts from the rear part of the skate and ends at its tip. After the push-off, the leg is fully tensed so that the body weight is transferred on to the other heavily bent leg, which is making the rearwards movement. The push-off leg follows the movement so that both skates come parallel with each other and execute a double curving movement (see Picture Series 2).

Picture Series 2

When skating backwards in a curve, both legs stay in contact with the ice. However, bio-mechanical analysis of top players show that some players lift the push-off leg a little after the push-off and then set it down again on the ice parallel with the other leg. Other players in this category lift the heel up high, leaving the tip of the skate still in contact with the ice the whole time.

Skating backwards - the most important points

Basic Position

- Bent knee
- Head and body lifted upright
- Broad leg split
- Body weight distributed over the complete skate runners
- Stick held in one hand in front of the body

Cycle: Push-off - Gliding - Push-off

- Alternate bending and tensing of the leg at the knee-joint
- Push-off (foot - heel - tip of the foot)
- Transfer the body weight onto the heavily bent leg (not onto the push-off leg)

Tips on Methods/Main Emphasis in Training

Skating backwards is not as simple as skating forwards, and because of this, skating forwards must be well learnt beforehand. Nevertheless, the training for the technique and the exercises are similar to those for skating forwards.

- Correct basic position.
- Balancing exercises on the spot - standing on one leg, knees bent, transferring the weight from one leg onto the other, bending forward, jumps and hops etc.
- Skating backwards on the ice with and without assistance of a partner, going along using the barrier (holding it with one hand) (see Diagram 22).

Diagram 22

- Skating backwards with a partner - the players stand opposite each other holding two sticks each. The person skating backwards is being pushed by the other, who has his knees slightly bent. The skates are kept at hips-width, the body weight is distributed over the right and left leg, the player glides on one leg etc. It is important with this exercise that the head is alternately looking in the direction being skated (see Diagram 23).

Diagram 23

- Skate backwards on both legs having pushed-off from the barrier (see Diagram 24), then followed by doing the knees bend, transferring the weight etc.

Diagram 24

- Skate backwards on one leg (see Diagram 25).

Diagram 25

- Now it's time to practice the **push-off and gliding** - the double snake shape - or the "fish" as it's sometimes called - is the starting point for this (just like in skating forwards). To learn this you begin in the basic position, the heels are turned outwards and the skates are set down on the inside edge of the runner. The knees are turned in towards each other and the pelvis is pushed to the rear. After the push-off, skate a curve on both legs back into the basic position. The exercise is done by using the knees, and without having to put a lot of energy into it (see Diagram 26). The most common mistake is to do too rapid and too short a curve, one after the other, and to bend the legs incorrectly (vertical movement of the center of balance of the body).

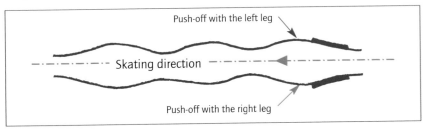

Diagram 26

The next exercise is doing the snake shape parallel, which is done by pushing-off from the inside edge of the left skate. The push-off is achieved by tensing the leg at the knee and moving the corresponding shoulder and hip to the rear. After the push-off the body weight is transferred onto the bent, right leg (not the push-off leg) and then the push-off leg (left) is pulled in towards the other leg. When skating backwards, the broader outside curve is typical for the tracks that are left behind (see Diagram 27).

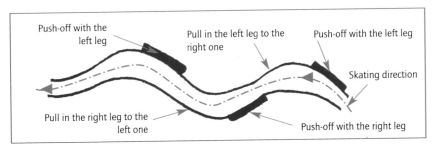

Diagram 27

Both exercises are done, first of all, with the assistance of a partner and then, later on, alone.

• Now, skating backwards from the basic position. Some Canadian authors call this movement from the push-off the C-Curve (see Diagram 28).

Diagram 28

It is recommended that the exercise is done with a partner first of all (see Diagram 29).

Diagram 29

- Finally, the C-Curve is combined with the cycle 'push-off - glide - push-off', remembering to take care to maintain a correct rhythm (see Diagram 30).

Diagram 30

The Main Mistakes in Technique

- The push-off is done from the tip of the skate and not from edge of the skate runner.
- Too stiff a basic stance (the trunk of the body is far too upright and the legs are held too tensely).
- Trunk of the body is held too far forward.
- The vertical hip movement is made too strongly.
- The motion is made too much by the legs and not by the hips and the shoulders.
- The curves are made too fast and too short without a gliding phase.

BRAKING AND STOPPING

The player needs this ice hockey skill in particular to slow down the skating speed and for changing direction. Players must be quite capable of being able to brake and stop quickly and safely. In actual play, braking, of course, is combined with the requirement to move off again (mainly using a starting movement). This is why, right from the beginning and as soon as the basic technique of braking and stopping has been learned, we always insist on a requirement to skate on in a certain direction or other.

Depending on the direction being skated, logically there are two variations of braking; braking **when skating forwards** and **braking when skating backwards**.

When **skating forwards** we talk of:

- the one-sided plough (one skate is turned inwards and dug in against the direction of skating).
- the full plough (with both skates turned inwards and dug in against the direction of skating).
- the swinging stop on both legs.
- the swinging stop on the inside leg.
- the swinging stop on the outside leg.

When **skating backwards** we talk of:

- the full plough on both legs (a V-stop).
- the one-sided plough on one leg.
- a swinging side stop on both legs.

Braking when Skating Forwards

Correct Technique

- The simplest way to stop is the **one-sided plough**. For this method, first of all the body weight is transferred over the gliding leg (e.g., the left one). The other (the right) is pushed a little forward, and with the tip of the skate turned inwards it is then placed down on the ice. The weight of the body is then transferred slowly onto the right leg until one comes to a halt. Both knees are bent. The trunk of the body must not be bent forward, and the right shoulder rotates slightly forward and the left one is pulled backwards (see Diagram 31).

Diagram 31

- In the **full plough** the tips of the skates on both legs are turned inwards at the same time. The heels are pulled outwards slowly, and the hips sink lower down with the knees pressing together against each other. Both skates start to glide. To come to a stop, the heels are pushed further outwards. The weight of the body is distributed evenly on both legs. The legs are bent at the knee and are relatively far apart from each other, and the body is well-balanced (see Diagram 32).

Diagram 32

- When **coming to a halt with a two-legged swing**, first of all the body and, of course, the skates must be unweighted. Skates, hips and shoulders are placed at a right angle to the direction being skated. The movement ends up with a sinking down of the body (done by bending the knees) and the finish of the digging in of the edges of the skates. The knees are pressed down towards the ice and at the same time into the tips of the skates (see Diagram 33). The braking energy is distributed evenly onto both skates held about hips-width apart, nevertheless the tips of the feet are well loaded (see Diagram 34).

Diagram 33

Diagram 34

- **Picture Series 3** shows the complete sequence of movements for coming to a stop with the swing on both legs.

Stopping on one leg when skating forwards requires certain skating experience. When stopping on the inside skate (right leg), the body weight is transferred on to the bent, left leg while the right leg is held to the rear, loosely above the ice. The tip of the skate on the right leg is turned outwards and brought towards the left leg in a T-position so that the right heel comes behind the left standing leg. The right skate is set down on the ice on its outside edge and at the same time the weight of the body is transferred to the right leg, which is tensed against the skating direction. The left leg lifts up off the ice and the whole body is held upright (see Diagram 35).

Diagram 35

The **swinging stop on the outside leg** is similar to the same type of movement described for the swinging stop on both legs. However, in this case the free leg helps to keep the balance and this partially makes the braking movement easier. This way of stopping is very efficient, particularly when the player might need to to start off again immediately in any direction (see Diagram 36).

Diagram 36

Tips on Methods/Main Emphasis in Training

* The first phase is the exercising of the one-sided plough on the spot. This involves placing the leg forward and turning it, with the body weight transferring onto that leg. At the same time the skate is doing the plough with the inside edge of the runner placed on the ice.
* The next step is learning the one-sided plough on the move (run-up with three steps). Of course you practice this on both legs.
* Then you do the movements with the tip of the skate towards the inside and the heel turned to the outside. You do the exercise standing and facing the barrier, where young players can hold on safely to the bar with two hands.
* The full plough is also done with a small run-up, and where the unweighting is emphasized followed by bending the knees. When doing this, the knees are pressed together. This type of braking is not particularly suitable for young players, however, because there is a high danger of injury.
* When the full plough has been mastered, you can begin with exercising the **swinging side stop on both legs**. In the beginning phases, it is important to concentrate on unweighting and turning the hips. At the same time bending the knees and the transfer of the body weight on to the front part of the skates will be practiced. Training for this is also done with a short run-up, which can be gradually lengthened. Attention must be paid to achieving sufficient pressure on the edge of the skate runners. It is important that the outside skate is braked using the inside edge and vice-versa, and that the pressure is maintained on the forward part of the skate. Just like the cross-over, when exercising the stop it is necessary to prefer doing it on the "easier, more comfortable" side. When the skill has been mastered on this one side then practice on both sides must be carried out.
* The correct braking technique can be improved by using different pieces of equipment and aids (see Diagram 37).
* As a last exercise, stopping on one leg (outside or inside) must be practiced. This skill must be mastered equally on both legs.

Diagram 37

The Main Mistakes in Technique

One-sided plough
- Trunk of the body bent too far forward.
- The weight is brought too quickly onto the braking leg.
- Skates are too far apart.
- The skate being braked is put down on the ice on its outside edge.
- The heel is not turned to the side enough.

The full plough
- The heel is not turned to the side enough.
- The knees are not bent enough.
- The knees are too far apart.
- The skates are being braked on the outside edge.

The swinging side stop on both legs
- The skates are not unweighted enough.
- The knees are not bent enough.
- The skates are not angled enough against the ice.
- Not enough pressure has been applied to the front part of the skates.

Braking when Skating Backwards

Correct Technique

- **Braking and stopping on both legs (the full plough)** is done by doing the splits and at the same time turning the tips of the skates outwards and applying pressure to the inside edge of the skates. Placing the skates down and stopping relies on unweighting the rear skate and by transferring the weight of the body on to the tips. When braking, a sideways pressure applied by the knees hard against the skating direction and pushing the tips of the skates further apart from each other helps. In this position the player ends up almost doing the wide version of the splits. Stopping is achieved by doing a deep knees-bend in the direction of the ice (see Diagram 38). This version is also sometimes called the V-Stop, like its description indicates.

Diagram 38

- **Braking and stopping on one leg** is done similarly to the one-sided plough in skating forwards. When skating backwards on both legs the braking leg (e.g., the left one) is lifted slightly clear of the ice by doing a little bend of the knee and then it is placed back down again to the rear. The tip of the skate is turned outwards. Then the leg is placed so that the skate is on its inside edge on the ice, against the skating direction. The weight of the body is now transferred onto the leg and the plough action creates the braking power. The gliding leg (right) goes into a deep knees-bend and stays on the ice (see Diagram 39). The legs end up in the so-called T-position, which permits an easy option to be able to move forward again.

Diagram 39

- Stopping using the swinging side stop on both legs occurs when skating backwards at speed and when the player wishes to move off again in a sideways direction. This version is the most difficult of all the braking techniques for skating backwards. The technique is the same as for skating forwards. It is particularly relevant that rapid unweighting of the body is achieved by energetically turning the head, shoulders and hips. This permits the skates to be unweighted and placed in a right-angled position against the direction being skated. The actual stop is achieved by lowering the center of balance and activating a slight pressure on the ice at the same time (with the outside edge of the inside skate and the inside edge of the outside skate). The knees are pressed down towards the ice and the skates are about hips-width apart (see Diagram 40).

Diagram 40

Tips on Methods/Main Emphasis in Training

- Practicing the stop when skating backwards should be done first after braking and stopping moving forwards has been mastered.
- In the first phase exercises at the barrier, grabbing it with both hands should be done (turning the skate tips outwards, bending the knees, doing the splits).
- Then do exercises with a partner. The braking player is in the braking position and the other player is skating forwards and is pushing the backwards skater gently and is helping him to keep his balance. The correct position of the legs is important here as well as a slightly bent forwards trunk of the body. The knees are being pressed down towards the ice (see Diagram 41).

Diagram 41

- The next part of the exercise is the actual stopping when skating backwards on your own. If a stick is being carried, this is held firmly in one hand.
- Braking on one skate is carried out right through to the end position – the so-called T-position – and this represents the position where you are ready to skate off again.
- When these techniques have been well mastered, you then will learn stopping using the swinging side stop on both legs. As training progresses, the speed of skating can be increased gradually. The exercise is to be practiced with both legs and each time is followed by skating off in the new direction.

The Main Mistakes in Technique

Stopping on both legs

- The tips of the skates are not turned outwards enough.
- The trunk of the body is not leaning far enough forward, so that the head is not held forward enough.
- The knees are not being pushed down towards the ice.
- Braking uses the whole length of the runner and not just only the inside edge.

Stopping on one leg

- The braking leg is weighted too quickly and too hard.
- Knees are not bent enough.
- The skates are too far apart.

Stopping using the swinging side stop on two legs.

- The body is not unweighted enough.
- Knees are not bent enough.
- Pressure is not applied to the forward part of the skate.

5 SKATING IN A CURVE

I n ice hockey, changing direction is done by skating in a curve and doing the cross-over. In order to increase speed in the curve, the cross-over should be integrated into it or the speed set at the start. A good ice-skater will also use the cross-over in a tight curve. The simplest method of changing direction, which beginners should learn, is skating in a curve. In practice this skill replaces even stopping.

Correct Technique

The body is bent forward in the middle of the curve. The inside shoulder is leant into the center of the curve. Both legs are bent and the weight of the body is held mainly over the inside, forward leg. The stick is held in both hands. To skate a left-handed curve the left leg is partially held forward of the right one (the distance between them should be about the length of a skate), and the weight of the body is held more over the left leg. The legs are bent at the knees, and at the center of the curve (to the left) the body is turned inwards. By shifting

Diagram 42a

the ankle the left skate moves onto the outside edge and the right one onto the inside edge. The right shoulder is brought forward and the left one is pulled back (in the middle of the curve). The tighter the curve, the more the inside leg is pushed forward, and the weight of the body is shifted into the center of the curve (see Diagram 42a) - which is accompanied by the skate being inclined the steepest to the ice during the movement. A good player can sometimes manage to brake lightly in a tight curve. Nevertheless, the movement should not be carried out too energetically. The weight of the body is distributed onto the tips of the skates so that the heels can glide along. At the end of the curve, you push-off again energetically in a new direction.

Diagram 42b

A recommendation for further phases of learning the technique of skating in a curve is to do exercises on the outside and inside edge of one skate (left and right leg). In order to be able to represent what is meant, the curves carried out on one skate (the one on the right leg) are described as **forward to the outside** and **forwards to the inside**. These exercises are very actual as the movements occur regularly in ice hockey.

The **forwards to the outside curve** - is learnt first of all without a stick. Once you can do the exercise well then it can be practiced with a stick. Starting from the basic position, the push-off is done on the inside edge of the left skate with the actual curve being done on the outside edge of the right skate. During the first half of the curve, the left leg is carried behind the body, slightly just above the ice. The back is turned towards the center of the curve and the left arm is held behind the body. In the second half of the curve, the free leg is brought forward alongside the right leg. The axis of the shoulders is twisted a little so that the right arm comes behind the body and the left arm is forward of the body. In the last phase the legs are brought together with, finally, a push-off with the right leg. The following curve is done on the outside of the left skate.

The forwards to the inside curve. The push-off is made with the inside of the left skate from the basic position. In the first half of the curve, the push-off leg (the left one) stays behind the body. The gliding (right) leg does a regular curve on the inside edge. The shoulders and the pelvis are at right angles to the skating direction with the right arm stretched out forwards. In the second part of the curve the push-off leg is brought forward alongside the standing leg. At this moment the left arm is laid across the back of the body while the right one is stretched out forwards. During the whole exercise, pay attention to the correct bending of the standing leg and maintain a regular speed when doing all the movements.

A good start for the effective training of the backward skated curve is naturally the mastering of being able to skate backwards well. Learning to do backward skated curves is the starting point for learning the backwards skated cross-over. The movements of the technique for the backwards skated curve to the outside are the same as those for backwards skating, with the difference, however, that the skates are held closer together. It is also important to make sure you bend the standing leg sufficiently and have sufficient inclination to the ice in the middle of the curve.

Tips on Methods/Main Emphasis in Training

There are two variations of skating in a curve. The first variant, which is not complicated to learn, involves changing direction by carrying out a wide curve. The second variant is where the curve is skated tightly and in which the player brakes slightly. This movement is one of the more demanding skills. Learning it requires a relatively long period of practice time with the requirement to constantly correct the technique. When exercising, you should begin with the easier leg (usually the left) and without a stick. When you have mastered this side, then you can practice the other leg. The exercise is always carried out on the move.

- The first phase of learning is being able to use the correct shoulder position and how this influences the curve. In this way, children learn that a change in the stance of the upper body has a considerable influence on the direction being skated. The curve is done on both skates with the arms held out to the sides. Only moving the shoulders and the arms changes the skating direction

(by rotating them to the sides - one arm comes into a rear position and the other in front of the body). Care should be taken from the beginning to ensure that the inside leg always stays to the rear.

- The second phase involves moving the shoulders and gently bending the body forwards, whereby the body weight is distributed slightly onto the inside leg (see Diagram 43). The curve is executed on the edges of both runners (see Diagram 44).

Diagram 43

Diagram 44

- Further, you now have to move the inside leg forward and at the same time bend it (see Diagram 45). Looking in the direction that is being skated makes this exercise easier.

Diagram 45

- Now practice skating in curves round cones, whereby the distance between the cones is shortened bit by bit (see Diagram 46).

Diagram 46

- After mastering the technique of doing the cross-over in a forwards direction, now use it when doing each curve (see Picture Series 4).

Picture Series 4

The Main Mistakes in Technique

- The basic mistake is when doing the curve on the outside leg because the inside leg is often incorrectly held behind the outside one.
- The inside leg is not bent at the knee and is not pushed forward enough, the body is held upright (this occurs through the movement on the heel of the inside leg).
- The body is not in the middle of the curve.
- The weight of the body is held over the heels.
- The skates are following each other too closely in the same track, which leads to a loss of balance.
- The exercises are carried out standing still too much - the player must always be moving along a little.
- The curve is not followed by doing a cross-over or a push-off.

6 THE CROSS-OVER FORWARDS

Correct Technique

As already mentioned, exercising of the forwards cross-over usually begins with practicing the left side. The movement stems from the hips and the pelvis is lifted up always. In order to be able to represent the movement better, the technique will be comprehensively described using the left-hand side. The left shoulder is pulled backwards and the right one forwards. The center of balance of the body is laid towards the middle of the curve. The skate of the outside leg (the right leg) is touching the ice on its inside edge, and the inside leg (the left one) is touching the ice with its outside edge. The push-off is carried out on the whole of the inside edge of the right (outside) skate. The weight of the body is on the well bent, left (inside) leg. The left skate is on its outside edge on the ice and moves in a curve. Now you cross-over, leading with the tip of the left skate across the right leg. Then you push-off with the outside edge of the left skate in the cross-over behind the right leg (see Diagram 47).

Diagram 47

After the push-off, the left leg is, so to speak, in the basic position, as it takes a fresh step forward. The right leg is gliding on its inside edge as it goes round the curve. The cycle of push-off - gliding - push-off is continually being repeated. A proper push-off can only be done with the whole of the outside edge of the runner on the inside skate. Player often tend to do the push-off incorrectly using the outside leg, so that the push-off with the inside leg is never completed fully. This results in a lack of rhythm and the movement ending up too slow. Therefore, according to how well this skill of pushing off with the inside edge is executed, one can measure the quality and speed of skating. Picture Series 5 shows the sequence of movements for the forwards cross-over.

Picture Series 5

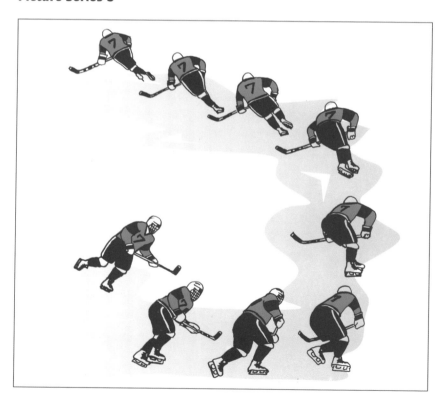

Players, who use the push-off correctly from the inside leg, are amongst the quickest ice-skaters. A firm, strong push-off from the inside leg, with a good co-ordinated hip movement, helps when moving forward and to be able to achieve the correct distribution of the weight of the body on to the outside leg.

Cross-over forwards – the most important technical points

Basic Position

- Hold body more upright.
- Bent knees.

Cycle: Push-off - Gliding - Push-off

- Alternate push-off from the outside and the inside leg and the edge of the skate runner.
- After the push-off from the outside leg the weight of the body is centered over the inside leg, which is well bent at the knee.
- The outside edge of the inside skate is on the ice and moves in a curve.
- The outside leg is crossed over the tip of the skate of the inside leg and placed down on the ice so that a push-off from the inside edge is possible.
- The push-off is ended on the outside edge of the skate on the inside leg, and a step is taken forwards.
- The outside leg moves in a curve on the inside edge of the skate.

Tips on Methods/Main Emphasis in Training

- Individual exercises in crossing over forwards can be carried out at the center face-off circle, which is ideal for this.
- The first skill that has to be learnt in crossing over forwards is to be able to skate **forwards in a circle** (without using the cross-over). Important here is using the correct rotation of the shoulders, and the positioning of the pelvis and skates. The shoulders and pelvis are turned into the middle of the circle. The edges of the outside and inside skate are slightly inclined towards the ice (in the direction of the center of the circle). The exercises are carried out first of all without a stick. When moving left, the right arm has to be held forward and the left arm behind the body.
- The second phase involves skating on the inside skate and exercising the push-off from the outside leg - the so-called **half skating step** or the 'skateboard pedal'. When skating to the left, the left leg is slightly bent at the knee and the weight of the body is centered over it. The push-off is carried out on the inside edge of the right skate. At the same time the left knee is bent and the right leg comes forward. Following this, the left leg is gradually stretched out and the right one is pulled forward on the ice alongside the left standing leg - the movement resembles the pedalling done on a skateboard. It is important to remember

Diagram 48

not to lift the left leg off the ice, but instead to hold the knee bent and keep the pelvis leaning forward all the time. The exercise is, of course, carried out on both sides.

- The next phase is the **switchover**, which merely serves as an excellent way of preparing for the cross-over. The skates are alternately lifted up off the ice. The leg that is at any one time above the ice is then placed down onto the ice next to the gliding, standing leg. The body is leaning slightly forward and the center of balance tends to lean towards the center of the circle. When skating left the push-off is done from the right (outside) leg, the left leg is lifted off the ice and placed down next to the right leg in the skating direction, the tips of the skates are not turned in or out at all. This exercise must also be practiced to the left and right.

- Next we come to the actual cross-over (a sideways crossing movement). This involves crossing the one leg over the other and placing the outside (right) skate on to the ice (see Diagram 48). First of all it is practiced standing still - children can keep hold of the side barrier rail. The outside (right) leg is lifted off the ice and crosses over the tip of the inside (left) skate. When doing this the skate is turned slightly towards the inside and is placed down on the front of the skate (see Diagram 49).

Diagram 49

- When the two previous phases have been mastered, you can then do the push-off with the inside leg. This exercise is not so easy and therefore it should be practiced holding the barrier rail first. In this case, the right, gliding leg is on the ice and the left leg pushes off from the outside edge in the cross-over behind the right leg and comes back into the normal position as quickly as possible (see Diagram 50). After learning this, the exercise is done on the move without holding on to anything. Again practice this on both sides equally.

Diagram 50

- Now practice each individual phase together in a sequence. It is recommended to start with a left-handed circle. The push-off is the same from the outside (right) skate as for the inside (left) skate. Keep looking at the inside of the circle. **Both legs must maintain the cycle rhythm push-off - glide - push-off.**
- The last phase involves maintaining the correct rhythm. The cross-over is usually practiced using an acoustic signal (numbers, clapping).

The Main Mistakes in Technique

- Knees not bent enough or not bent at all.
- The push-off from the inside leg is insufficient and too small a skating step forward is used.
- The push-off from the inside and the outside leg is not balanced ('limping' motion).
- Placing the skate down on the heel and not on its tip.
- When crossing over, the knee of the outside leg is fully stretched out.
- The cycle rhythm push-off - glide - push-off is not maintained - one tends to jump.
- The gliding phase is not the same on the right and left skate.
- The center of balance is not distributed enough sideways (into the center of the circle).
- The back of the body is facing into the center of the circle.

THE CROSS-OVER BACKWARDS

This is not quite an easy skill to master and makes various different demands on the player. It is essential to be capable of mastering good skating, in particular skating in a circle backwards.

Correct Technique

The center of weight of the body is leaning more towards the center of the circle with the knees bent and the body and head held more upright. Lifting and lowering the pelvis has a positive effect on the push-off.

In the backwards cross-over to the left, the right leg is always crossed over the left leg. The push-off occurs from the outside edge of the left (inside) skate in a way that the last phase of the push-off is done from the tip of the skate. The weight of the body is centered over the right (outside) leg with its knee well bent, and which is gliding round the curve in front of the inside (left) leg. The inside leg is bent after the push-off and then the outside leg crosses over the axis of the left leg. Finally then there is the push-off from the inside edge. Balance is maintained by the knee being well bent. The whole sequence of the movement is shown in Picture Series 6.

Cross-over backwards - the most important technical points

Basic Position

- The body is held more upright.
- The knees are bent.

Cycle: Push-off - Gliding - Push-off

- The push-off occurs alternately from the inside and then the outside leg.
- The push-off from the inside leg is done from the outside edge of the tip of the skate.
- The weight of the body is centered over the outside leg (which is gliding round the curve).
- The outside leg is placed over the axis of the inside leg and is followed by a push-off from the inside edge.

Tips on Methods/Main Emphasis in Training

- In the event there is a similar methodical sequence used as in the cross-over forwards.
- The first phase is skating backwards in a circle to the left without a stick and after a run up (legs are not used). It is important to adopt the correct body posture - knees slightly bent, center of balance is leant towards the center of the curve, the left arm is held loosely behind the body, the right one is on the other side (in front of the body). The whole exercise is carried out with the legs in a parallel, hips-width position.
- The next exercise is the half skating step or the 'skateboard pedal' backwards. The basic position is the same - the push-off is done from the inside edge of the right skate with its tip turned inwards. After the push-off, the right leg is brought round in a curve on the ice into the basic position. The gliding phase is used to its fullness and the push-off repeated. The exercise is done on both sides but also with the stick.
- As preparation for the cross-over, the switchover is practiced. This exercise is done first of all standing at the barrier rail and later on the move. The sequence of the exercise is the same as that for the forwards cross-over. Both skates are lifted alternately up off the ice and then put back down again close to the gliding, standing leg.
- For the crossing over of the legs you start practicing at the barrier rail. Here it is emphasized that the knees must be bent (in this position they are quite

Picture Series 6

close together). The push-off leg is bent after the push-off, and the outside leg is placed over the axis of the inside leg and pushes off from the inside edge.

- How the push-off from the inside leg is carried out is demonstrated at the barrier rail. The knees are bent, and the left leg is crossed over behind the left one in order to push-off from the whole of the outside edge of the skate (on the left leg). After the push-off, the left leg (stretched out) is lifted up from the ice and brought by the shortest route alongside the gliding leg (in the cross-over). The exercise is practiced, of course, on both sides.

- Now it's time for the backwards cross-over in a circle, remembering all the points described already. The sequence of movements is practiced again on both sides with and without the stick (see Diagram 51). It has proved to be helpful to do the exercise with a partner. The skater moving forwards holds the backwards skater by the forearms. Later on you practice on your own, however first of all at a slow speed.

- The last phase is to concentrate on the correct rhythm of the cross-over.

Diagram 51

The Main Mistakes in Technique

- Incorrect basic position - body leaning over too much, head not held upright.
- When crossing over the legs they are stretched out and not bent.
- Unequal push-off from both legs.
- Incorrect placement of the inside skate on the ice after the push-off from the outside leg - the inside leg is turned too little (there is a slight braking effect when the skate is placed down on the ice).
- The push-off is done using only the tip of the skate and not in the sequence with the whole of the edge of the skate ending up on the tip of the skate.
- The push-off movements are done too quickly one after the other, and as a result the gliding phases are not used to best effect.

TURNS

Turns play a very important role in ice hockey, particularly when changing direction. There are two different sorts:

- Turn to skate backwards when skating forwards
- Turn to skate forwards when skating backwards

Turns are carried out, of course, in both directions and either on one leg or on both. When doing this, it is important to maintain a skating rhythm and at the same time not let the speed drop. After the turn, you skate away increasing your speed (just like after you have done a stop).

Correct Technique - Turning from Skating Forwards into Skating Backwards

Beginners practice two different versions. The first version is doing the turn on one or both legs. The second version is switching over from one leg onto the other leg (also sometimes called the 'Mohawk'). The technicalities of doing both versions can be divided into three phases:

- Unweighting
- Turning
- Dropping down

Turning on Both Skates

One should begin by learning this simple version. The starting position is by skating forwards on both legs with the knees slightly bent. When turning left the ska-

tes are unweighted by bringing the body upright. At the same time the right shoulder is brought quickly forward and the left one to the rear. The hips move in the same way so that, by virtue of these movements through the tips of the skates, you find your- self skating backwards. The legs

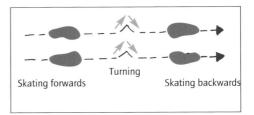

Diagram 52

are then bent at the knees (the center of balance drops downward) in order to gain stability for skating backwards further. The principle behind this turn lies in the unweighting of the skates and then the energetic movement of the shoulders and the hips. The tracks on the ice are shown in Diagram 52.

Turning on One Skate

This version of turning is used in the game at a moment when the player is alrea- dy skating forwards on one skate and is forced to turn to skate backwards. The cy- cle of the movements is the same, but it is important to begin on the bent leg with an unweighting following this, as well as the energetic motion of the shoulders and the hips.

In both versions of the turn it seemingly often occurs that when the skate is un- weighted a little jump happens. In order to maintain your balance, it is important to bend the knees after the turn.

Turning by Changing over from One Leg to the Other

It is recommended that you practice this version after the two previous exerci- ses have been mastered. When turning to the right, the bent left leg is placed forwards while the shoulders and the hips are turned fiercely to the right. At the same time the rear, right leg is unweighted. The right leg is pulled along- side the left, gliding leg and the tip of the skate is turned outwards (the heels

Diagram 53

are together). After placing the foot down, and as you transfer the weight of the body onto the right leg, you will find that the legs are seemingly quite wide apart and then you move into a backwards gliding phase (see Diagram 53).

Picture Series 7 shows the whole sequence of movements for the turn from skating forwards into skating backwards.

Turning in a Curve

This turn is often used in play by defenders. The player is skating forwards with bent legs and pushes one leg forward. In a turn to the right, the right skate is brought slightly forward of the left one, so that gliding into a right-handed curve begins. At the point where the middle of the curve is reached, you unweight yourself with an energetic motion of the hips and shoulders into the opposite direction. The left shoulder is brought slightly to the rear and the right one forward. The left skate points slightly forwards and does a tight curve backwards on the outside edge, while the right skate is moving along on its inside edge.

At high speed, when there isn't time to do a wider curve at the mid-point, you brake slightly in order to carry out the turn in the same way as described above.

Picture Series 7

Correct Technique - Turning from Skating Backwards into Skating Forwards

Here, there are usually three different turn versions used.

Turning on Both Skates

The method of doing this turn is the same as the turn when skating forwards. So, when gliding forwards on both legs, with knees slightly bent, the skates are un-weighted by a lifting of the weight of the body with the knees and the pelvic region. Just before you go into the actual turn, the trunk of the body, shoulders and head are turned quickly into the new skating direction. Thus the turn that follows, and which is done more on the tips of the skates, is made much easier. In order to avoid losing speed and the rhythm of the movements, the motions carried out by the legs, trunk of the body and shoulders have to be completed at the same time.

Turning by Changing over from One Leg to the Other

When turning left while skating backwards, the weight of the body is centered over the right leg with the knee bent. The left leg is lifted up and bent with the tip

Diagram 54

of the skate turned forwards in the skating direction. At this moment, the weight of the body is also transferred onto this leg. The head, trunk of the body and shoulders are brought into the direction of the turn with a simultaneous un-weighting of the hips. You then skate on (see Diagram 54).

A similar variation of the turn, which often occurs, is where shortly before doing the turn, the weight of the body is centered over the push-off leg by doing a cross-over. The sequence of subsequent movements is the same then as in the previous paragraph. This version of the turn is shown in Picture Series 8.

Picture Series 8

Tips on Methods/Main Emphasis in Training

The successful execution of the turns on one or both skates depends on a certain degree of skill and ice-skating prowess. When exercising it is best, first of all, to master one version before going on to practice the others. The following order of priority is recommended:

- Turn when skating forwards on both legs
- Turn when skating forwards using the switchover
- Turn when skating backwards on both legs
- Turn when skating backwards by using the cross-over
- Turn when skating forwards on one leg

When practicing without a stick, the following sequence has proved to be the best:

- The basic movement (unweighting, turning the tips of the skates, and lowering the center of balance) are all practiced standing front on holding on to the barrier rail.
- Next the turn is practiced on the spot and then at a slow speed. The basic position is adopted with slightly bent knees, one arm held forward and the other held behind the back. The arm behind the back is the one on which side you will be doing the turn. Once again it must be emphasized that the turn should be practiced using, first of all, your easier side. The turn is done with both skates with the weight of the body distributed evenly on both legs. This version of the turn also serves above all as practice for the switchover turn.
- Practicing the switchover turn starts, just like the previous exercise, standing at the barrier rail. Here you practice the rotation and placing the rear foot down. An important point is the 'rocking' movement when transferring from the forward foot to the rear foot - i.e., the motion of lifting the hips.
- In the second phase you practice the movements on the move skating slowly forwards. The tip of the skate of the rear leg is turned slightly to the rear, and a light braking on the inside edge (from the tip of the skate) is used to assist the movement. When the tip of the skate presses down onto the ice, you come

into a gentle turn in the planned direction. Afterwards the weight of the body moves over the rear leg, while at the same time, of course, the front leg is unweighted.

- After managing to do the turn on the rear leg successfully, the whole exercise is practiced together with the unweighting movements.
- The turns are done in both directions and with and without a stick.

The Main Mistakes in Training

- The turn is attempted without unweighting.
- Insufficient rotation of the trunk of the body and shoulders.
- The turn is done from the rear leg onto the front leg.
- When turning on both legs, the body is leaning backwards.
- When turning using the cross-over the foot is not placed down in the new direction.
- Failure to start skating off after the turn.
- Only practicing the exercise on one side.

9
STARTS

peed is one of the main characteristics of today's ice hockey game. Starting plays an important role in the game, above all in disengaging from the opposition, attack, change of direction and chasing the opponent. The technique of the start in ice hockey is built up on the same principles as it is in other types of sport. First of all there is a transfer of the center of balance in the direction of the start. The danger of overbalancing forward is avoided by taking short, quick and powerful skating steps forward. These steps turn gradually into long gliding ones. It is essential that a good player must be able to do the start from the standing position, while on the move (spurting) and from various other positions and circumstances. The following types of start are considered:

- The forwards start.
- The start backwards.
- The start sideways.
- Start in any direction after having stopped, off one leg and off both legs.

Practicing all the types is important for all age groups. Nevertheless, you can only begin with the training after you have mastered the skills of skating.

Correct Technique

Starting Forwards from a Normal Standing Position

This start is characterized by having the knees well bent and with the trunk of the body leaning forward. The tips of the skates are turned relatively wide outwards. The center of balance of the body is held forward and a possible tumbling over is compensated for by taking quick, short skating steps. Biomechanical studies show that the angle between the tips of the skates in the first four skating steps measures between 87° - 38° (see Diagram 55).

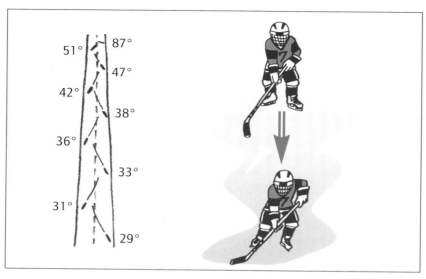

Diagram 55

The cycle – push-off/push-off – is done using the inside edge of the skate. First of all the steps taken are short ones, and later become longer ones until gliding steps are achieved. The body slowly comes into a more upright position. After an energetic push-off from the tip of the skate, it is placed down on the ice along the whole of the skate runner. The arm movements accompanying the motions also play an important role (see Diagram 56).

Diagram 56

Starting from a Sideways Position

The basic position is characterized by the legs slightly apart to one side and an upright body. In order to picture the sequence of movements better, we describe the start moving to the left. For the start, the push-off is done to the left from the whole length of the inside edge of the right (outside) skate. The weight of the body is centered over the left (inside) leg, which the right leg then crosses over. Following this there is a further push-off with the other leg (from the tip of the outside of the left skate), with a simultaneous frontal rotation of the body in the skating direction (see Diagram 57).

Diagram 57

Starting Forwards from a Skating Forwards Position

By bending the body more forwards, the player transfers the weight of the body also forwards. The legs compensate for this movement by taking shorter steps. The skate moves sideways in a tight snake shape (the 'S' snake shape described earlier is shortened). At the start, the skate is lifted off the ice slightly and set down again later on the whole length of the skate runner. The tip of the skate is then turned outwards. The remainder of the sequence of movements is the same as for the start forwards from a standing position.

Starting in the Opposite Direction from a Stop Position after Skating Forwards

With this version of the start it is relevant to differentiate whether it involves stopping on one (outside or inside) leg or on both legs. In both cases, dependant on which kind of stop is used, this leads to making best use of the backwards skating motion.

After stopping on the **outside leg**, one can usually use either start version. It is a question of starting from the 'T' position of the legs. The player tends to bend the knees and transfer the body weight on to the push-off leg - the one that is turned at right angles to the skating movement. The second skate is left pointing in the skating direction ('T' position), and with a simultaneous turning of the tip of the skate outwards. Then the **cycle push-off - push-off** follows as already described (see Diagram 58).

Diagram 58

The second version of the start is similarly based on the cross-over as in the start sideways.

When stopping on the inside leg, the starting technique is similar to the start from the standing position. The technical difference is that the weight of the body after stopping is on the inside leg and therefore the cross-over comes next and not after a push-off from the outside leg.

When stopping on both legs, two types of start are possible, and these have already been described in the section starting after stopping on one leg (see Diagram 59 and 60).

Diagram 59

Diagram 60

Starting Forwards from a Stop Position after Skating Backwards

When skating backwards the stop is achieved by doing the full plough, which has already been described. In the last phase the legs are wide apart with the tips of the skates turned outwards, the knees are bent and are being pushed down towards the ice. The whole body is leaning forwards - this ensures that a favorable biomechanical position for the next movement is gained. Then you do tight backward curves on both legs as both heels move together. The weight of the body is centered over the push-off leg with the tip of the skate on this leg being turned at a right angle to the direction of movement. The other leg is lifted up off the ice and is placed down again just as in the forwards start. Then follows the cycle push-off - push-off as already described (see Diagram 61).

Diagram 61

Starting from a Sideways Position after Skating Backwards

In this type of start, the body weight must first of all be placed over the push-off leg by doing a crossover movement. With reference to the side from which to start it will always be from the opposite leg.

When starting off to the left, you do a cross-over left and backwards, with the weight of the body on the right (push-off) leg. This leg is bent and the skate is tilted over towards the ice so that a good basis for the push-off is established. The other (left) leg is turned to the side after the cross-over and placed down on the ice in the skating direction. The weight of the body is transferred on to the left leg and the player skates or does cross-over steps forwards. The whole sequence of the technique is shown in Picture Series 9.

Picture Series 9

Tips on Methods

- Practice is only possible after all the basic ice-skating skills have been mastered.
- First of all, it is necessary to master the starts from a standing still position and then to combine the starts after stopping with starts on the move.
- Practice starts with turning the tips of the skates outwards and leaning over with the body. The center of balance is lowered and the knees are quite well bent. The exercise is carried out facing the barrier rail, holding on to it with both hands. It is important to make sure that placing the skate down on the ice is carried out correctly with its tip turned outwards (see Diagram 62).

Diagram 62

It is recommended that you do this exercise also with a partner. The player doing the exercise bends forward and pushes the other one, who brakes the movement. The exercise is excellent for learning to transfer the body weight forwards (falling forwards) and for learning how to set the skate down on the ice (see Diagram 63).

Diagram 63

- The next phase is to learn how to do the short steps when starting. All these exercises have to be practiced using the highest step frequency possible (for example the stamping step etc.).

- When you have mastered the correct angle of lea- ning the body forward and the high frequency of step, both of these can be integrated into the com- plete starting sequence. An important aspect is to learn how to lengthen your step. For this you usually use simple exercises. For example use ice hockey sticks lying on the ice at different intervals, which are laid out gradually further apart. The player has to use the gaps between the sticks and place one step in each gap (see Diagram 64).

Diagram 64

- The same kind of exercises is used when practicing the sideways start from a standing position. The player stands sideways to the direction to be skated and with one leg he steps over one of the sticks and then skates forward from here (see Diagram 65).

Diagram 65

- For this exercise it is important to breathe correctly at the same time.
- The last phase is to practice the starts in all directions from skating forwards and backwards.
- Practicing the starts is very energetic and exhausting and therefore should be practiced in short sessions (2-3, with pauses of 3-5 minutes between the sessions). The sessions should be repeated 4-6 times together with sufficient pauses between the repeats (1:8).

The Main Mistakes in Training

- Tips of the skates are not sufficiently turned outwards.
- The push-off is not done powerfully enough from the tips of the skates.
- The **cycle push-off - push-off** is lacking and the gliding phase is too long - the player takes too lengthy a step at too low a frequency.
- When starting, the body is not leaning forward enough and the knees are not bent enough.
- The length of the steps is not gradually increased and the gliding step is too long - **cycle push-off - gliding - push-off**.
- When starting sideways, the inside leg is not bent enough and the weight of the body is not transferred over the outside leg. At the same time, the push-off is not done from the tip of the skate on the inside leg.

10 SKILLFUL SKATING

The whole business of skating in ice hockey consists of a large number of movements that are used during the game, sometimes often and sometimes less often. Practicing all these movements, however, is not part of the basic training in ice-skating. It is assumed that, when training, the skills have been already learnt and these experiences are then combined with the movements and developed further.

This brings all the turns on either one or both feet, done with the cross-over, moving on to the next skating direction or moving on using the cross-over etc., into play. Included in this category is skating in a curve followed by the cross-over or braking etc. This also applies to all the changes of direction after stopping on one or both skates, starts, skating curves on the glide in combination with the cross-over. Thus it's all about certain maneuvers such as jumping and leaping, changing position like kneeling, lying down, bending the knees of one leg or both etc.

An overview shows clearly that the palette of skilled skating is quite wide and colorful. In order to be able to perfect skilled skating, however, the basics as described in the previous chapters (with and without a puck) have to be mastered.

One special area concerns ice-skating as a goalkeeper. The advice and methods on this subject are to be found in other publications.

The skills of ice-skating in ice hockey have to be mastered by any person wanting to become a player. Practicing and perfecting one's ice-skating is something that is never ending, and something which even the best players cannot do without in training. In the initial years of training, these activities will take up a considerable part of the exercising. One should use as large a spectrum of aids as possible. Poor ice-skating skills will, of course, limit the player and will prevent him being able to improve in the years that follow.

After mastering the basic techniques it is necessary to combine the movements and skills with other elements of the game - above all with managing the puck.

Practice shows that the business of ice-skating backwards and forwards with the puck, with rapid changes of direction, is often underestimated. This is a negative point in matches between countries that belong to the world's leaders in ice hockey. Especially for young players these exercise skills, with or without the puck, guarantee quality and firm movement stereotypes, and this leads eventually, by continuous repetition, to individual perfection.

In training, at all ages, exercises, involving a change of the center of balance (bending the knees low, kneeling, leaning forward) when controlling the puck, are often neglected. In today's game, which is characterized by a lot of body contact, mastering this particular skill is very important. The skill allows the player to keep the puck under control and able to permit a shot at goal from all the various game situations.

Premature specialization of a player as a defender or a forward at too early an age has a negative effect on mastering all of the ice-skating skills required. It prevents any further individual development of the necessary skills. In older players one often comes across unskillful and slow defenders and on the other hand forwards, all of which do not have a complete mastery of the defense skills.

In older age groups, only excellent, well-learnt ice-skating techniques, combining good puck control together with well developed speed, power and skill, will bring the players to be real champions and see advances. It must, however, be noted that rhythmical skating in long curves alone will not bring about the development of speed-skating. This skill can only be developed by carrying out rapid changes of direction when skating forwards and backwards and also when stopping.

Understanding and being able to put the described methods, specifics and patterns into practice will make itself felt in technically well-equipped players, who not only have a good playing performance, but who bring fun into the game.

11

LITTLE GAMES ON THE ICE

1. The players stand in a row along the goal line. A number is called out meaning the number of steps to be taken at the start. On the command, all the players move forward and, after the number of steps called out have been taken, carry on gliding on one leg. Whoever glides the farthest is the winner.

Variations:

a) Doing the same game but with bent knees.

b) Doing the game with one knee bent.

c) With leg stretched out backwards horizontally.

d) Less run-up steps are taken.

2. The players are divided up into two groups and stand on the sidelines of the rink opposite each other. The players of the one group all clasp each other's hands and on a command both groups skate towards each other. The group not holding hands skate under the joined hands of the other group. When doing this skating backwards the roles are changed.

3. Catching Games:

a) Play is done in a restricted area and one player is chasing another. If the first player is caught or is forced to leave the marked out area, the second player is the winner - roles are changed over.

b) Two players holding hands chase two others also holding hands. When they are caught they follow on behind. If the players chasing let go of their hands, a catch is invalid. If the players being chased let go of their hands, it automatically counts as being caught.

c) Three players take part:

- One player chases the other two.
- The first player starts off chasing the second player, who then chases the third player, who in turn chases the first player.

d) One or two players chase all the others.

e) In a laid down time (e.g., after 20 seconds), each player tries to catch as many other players he can.

f) The player being chased is holding an object (e.g., a glove, a puck, a ball...), which he has to pass on to the other players. The catcher can only catch someone who is holding the object.

g) The player being chased is on his own. The others are in twos (holding hands). Whoever gets caught takes on the chasing role and the catcher takes the partner.

4. A chosen player tries to catch his opposite number and thus gain a helper. The chasers and those being chased skate towards each on a command - those being chased can only avoid being caught by skating backwards. The chaser can only skate forwards. The game goes on until only one player remains and he becomes the first chaser in the next game.

5. The players are divided up into four groups. Each group is standing in the face-off circle. A 'magician' is standing in the center of the game holding a magician's 'wand'. When the 'magician' holds the 'wand' over his head all the players have to glide towards him with knees bent. As soon as the 'wand' is placed on the ice, all the players have to go back to the edge of the circle. The 'magician' chases them and whoever gets caught is the next 'magician'.

6. The groups (say two teams) stand in rows alongside each other. In front of each team, at a distance, there are three markers. Each team has three objects. At a command the first player in each team takes one of the objects to the first marker and skates back. He does the same with the other objects, once to the second marker and once to the third marker. At the clap of the hands, the next team player skates off and brings the objects (one after another) back to the start. The third player in each team then takes the objects out to the markers etc. The team that achieves the quickest change-over wins.

7. Relays:

a) The players stand lined up in teams. On the ice in front of each team there are three markers. At each marker, each of the players has to carry out a task laid down (do a turn, bend the knees, do a stop, carry out a jump etc.). Once the task is done he comes back and runs round his team and joins in at the back. Then the second player starts.

b) The teams stand in rows lined up. Hurdles have been placed out in front of each team. On a command individual players skate forward, jump over the hurdles and skate back again.

c) The teams stand in a circle with their left hips turned into the center of the circle. All the players receive a number. The first one has a relay baton. On a signal, the first one skates round the circle and hands the baton over to the second one. The team that gets all of its players home first wins.

d) The teams stand behind a line. On a signal, the first player skates off and around a cone back to his team. Here he gets hold of the second player around the hips and they skate off together round the cone. This carries on until the whole team is skating holding hips together. After that the same game is played starting with the whole team, but in the opposite direction. Each time the team reaches home, one player separates off and then next time a second player drops off.

e) The same as the previous game, except that skating to the cone is done through a slalom.

f) The players are in two groups standing on the blue line facing the goal. On a command, the first player skates through a figure of eight round the face-off circles (between the blue line and the goal) using the cross-over and hands on the baton at the end.

8. This game is suitable for total beginners. The players are divided into two groups - "Eagles" and "Hawks". A certain number of pucks ('eggs') are placed in two 'nests' (the face-off circles). At a signal, the two groups try to get as many 'eggs' into their own 'nest'. Body contact is permissible.

9. The following game concentrates on attentiveness and change of direction. The rink represents a ship on which fire has broken out. The players all carry out different tasks. On the command, "Fore!" everyone skates to the goal line, and on "Aft!" to the other end, then on the command "Cabin!" everyone lies on their stomach, and on "Fire on board!" everyone leaps up onto the barrier rail.

10. On a signal, the players skate from one "nest" to the other. As they do this they must not be caught by the "Pirates". The players may only skate forwards and sideways (not backwards). When they reach the "nest" they are in safety. Whoever is caught by the pirates, joins in as a pirate.

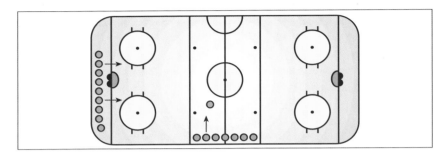

11. The players stand in two rows. The "Hunter" calls out, "Last pair forward" and they skate forward and try to join hands. If the "Hunter" catches someone, they change over roles.

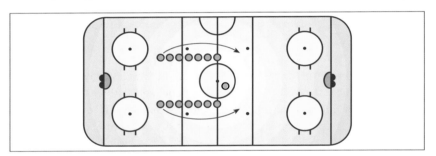

12. The players stand lined up at the center face-off circle in groups. On a command, each one tries to touch the end barrier rail as fast as possible. The winning team is the one that manages to line up at the center face-off circle first. The game can also be played using the side barrier rails.

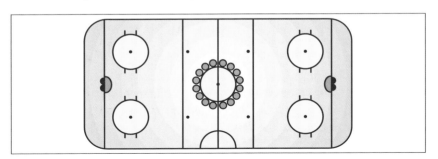

13. The players (divided up into two groups - "Reds" and "Blacks") are standing or sitting on the red line with their backs to each other. On the command "Red!", all the players of this group skate to a predetermined spot. As they do this, the second group tries to catch them. The number of caught players gives the number of points for that team. The winning team is the one with the most points at the end of the game.

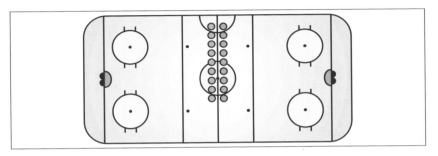

14. Each player is given a number.
a) The coach calls one out of two numbers. All the players with this number skate round the rink and try to be first back on their starting spot.
b) The numbers are distributed so that there are pairs. When the number is called out, both players skate off and try to take away objects lying between the two groups. The winner is the first to bring the object back to his group.

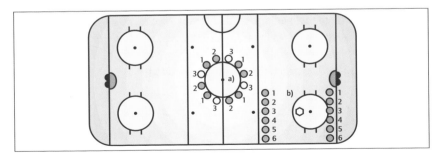

15. The players skate in rows behind each other and try to copy the leader as he does different movements, changes direction etc. The players can hold hands or each other by the hips as they skate.

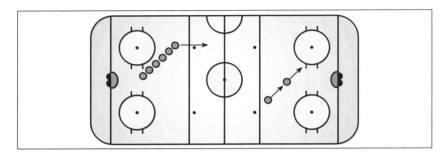

16. The coach uses different signals. When he gives a signal (say - holds his hand up) all the players skate forwards, and when he gives a different signal (say - hand on hip) then they do the cross-over to the side indicated etc.

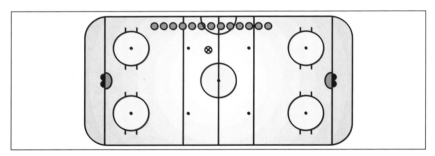

17. The players skate freely round the rink. When a signal is given they stop immediately and may not move. Whoever moves is given a penalty point.

18. The players are divided into rows of no more than 5 players. The first player in each row chases after the last man in the other row. The leader of the row being chased has to avoid his row being caught. The rows must not become separated.

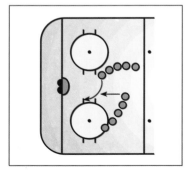

19. The players are divided into two teams (each 5 people) and form a row - "train". The man behind grasps the player in front round the hips. Like this the "train" moves forwards as each player pushes-off (using the same leg and the same amount of effort). The leading player is the "train driver" and determines which direction the train moves in.

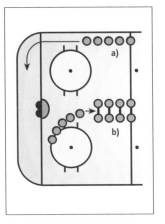

Variations:

    a) On a signal the "train" moves by only using the knees bend action.

    b) One group forms a tunnel and the others go through with knees bent.

20. The players being chased may only skate backwards in a restricted area. The chaser skates forwards with his arms linked behind his back. He can only catch someone by touching them with his head on their chests. Should one of the players being chased begin to skate forwards, then he becomes a chaser.

21. The players skate round the outside of the rink in a row at regular distances between each other. On a command, a player tries to catch the one skating in front of him without being caught by the man behind. If he fails to succeed, he gets a penalty point.

Variation:

The players (each time 4-6) skate around the center face-off circle. The game is played in both directions.

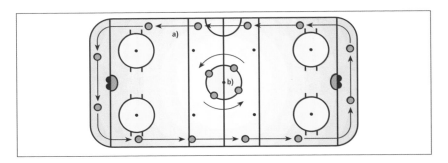

22. The players are standing in a row on the center line and hold hands (standing all forward in the same direction). On a signal, the teams skate as fast as possible round the two face-off circles on their side. The teams may not loosen hands as they do this.

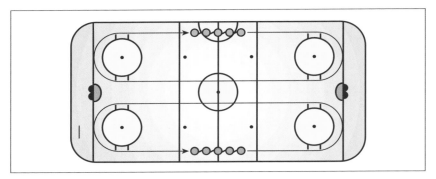

23. Four groups stand on the sides of an imaginary square. On a signal they have to skate to another spot on the square. They may skate in any direction (straight, diagonally, sideways).

24. The players are standing on the blue line facing the blue line at the other end. On a signal they skate to this blue line and on another signal they skate back. As they skate further signals are given and at each they have to change the skating direction. The players do not know which line is the final target.

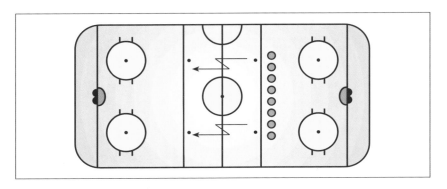

25. The players are standing in the center face-off circle in twos, one behind the other. One of these players is selected and chases the other player round the circle. The person being chased can save himself by standing in front of any couple in the circle. When this happens the rear player of this couple becomes the chaser and the previous chaser becomes the person being chased. If the chaser catches his man then the roles are changed over.

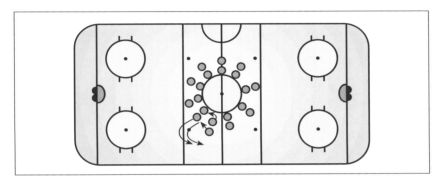

12
SKATING EXERCISES

Exercise 1

The players are in two groups in the opposite diagonal corners of the rink. The first group skates a slalom with tight curves. The second group skates forwards and changes over skating direction twice when between the inside area of the blue lines after stopping.

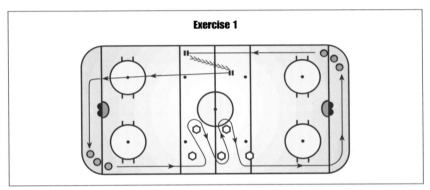

Exercise 1

Exercise 2

The players skate a slalom round the face-off circles at each opposing end of the rink. They skate back to the start along the barrier rail.

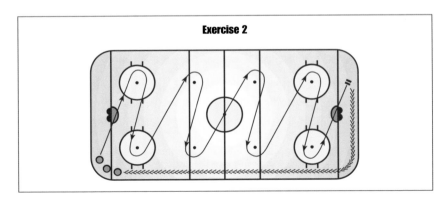

Exercise 2

Exercise 3

The players start off in the corners of the end zone. The first part of the slalom is skated using tight curves, and the second with the cross-over.

Exercise 4

The exercise concentrates on practicing the movements of skating forwards, backwards and sideways (for the cross-over).

Exercise 5

The players skate two rounds of the face-off circle, and then skate to the blue line and after stopping skate backwards to the barrier rail and behind the goal line back to the team.

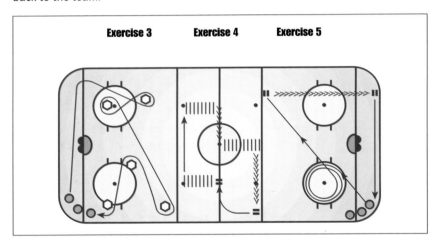

Exercise 6

Skate round the one face-off circle using the forwards cross-over and round the other using tight curves (in both directions).

Exercise 7

The players alternately jump over or go underneath the hurdles. Each time they skate back alongside the barrier rail.

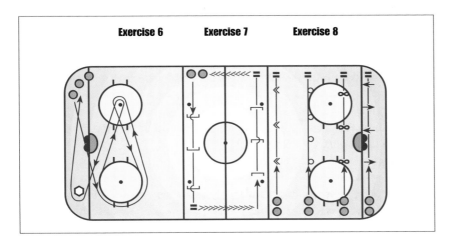

Exercise 8

The players do various different actions and skills (knee bending, jumping, turn, loop turns, kneeling etc.).

Exercise 9

The players are divided into teams of 5. Practice the forwards cross-over and backwards cross-over round a face-off circle. Do two circles in the same direction.

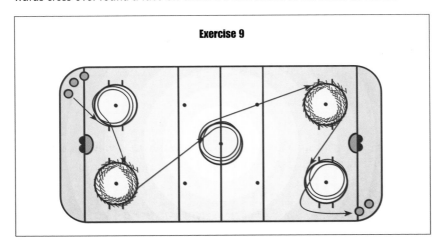

Exercise 10

The players are in two groups in the opposite diagonal corners of the rink. The first group skates forwards to the blue line, and on reaching the line skates sideways up to about the middle of the pitch and then continues on to the second blue line by skating forwards. They then skate sideways again and then forwards into the corner. The second group does the same route similarly, but instead of forwards they skate backwards.

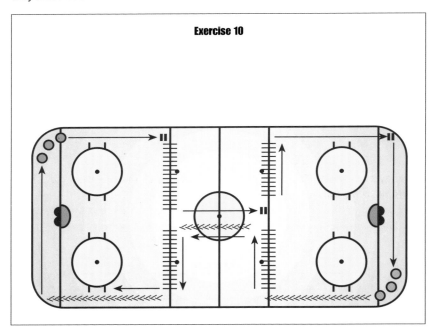

Exercise 10

Exercise 11

The players skate through a slalom with hurdles, which they jump over backwards and skate back to the start position.

Exercise 12

The players skate on the other side of the pitch using the forwards cross-over and skate back to the start position using the backwards cross-over.

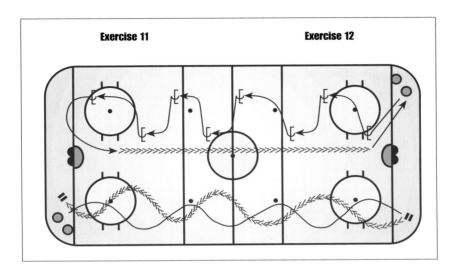

Exercise 11

Exercise 12

Exercise 13

The players skate forwards diagonally on the lines, at the end they skate backwards along the line.

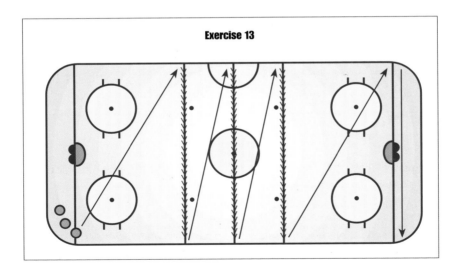

Exercise 13

Exercise 14
A slalom course with hurdles is skated alternately jumping over them and ducking under them.

Exercise 15
A slalom course with tight and wide curves round hurdles is skated jumping over them.

Exercise 16
A slalom course is set up to practice skills alternately from skating forwards, backwards and jumping over hurdles.

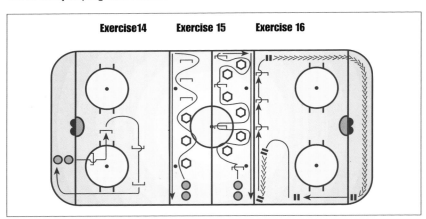

Exercise 14　　**Exercise 15**　　**Exercise 16**

Exercise 17
The players skate in tight curves round the cone.

Exercise 18
The course consists of hurdles that the players jump over on the first round and then on the second use as slalom turn points.

Exercise 19
The players skate in a slalom round the cones using tight curves.

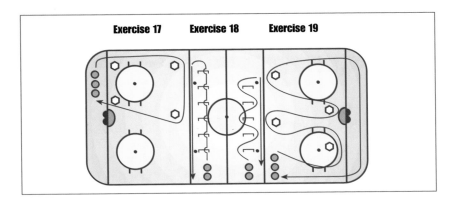

Exercise 17   **Exercise 18**   **Exercise 19**

Exercise 20
The players are in two groups. Little competitions are held skating round the cone using different skating motions (forwards, backwards etc.).

Exercise 21
The players skate forwards with the coach indicating in which direction the curve has to be skated.

Exercise 22
Two teams skate backwards to the blue line where they skate sideways while the other team practices forwards skating along the barrier rail line.

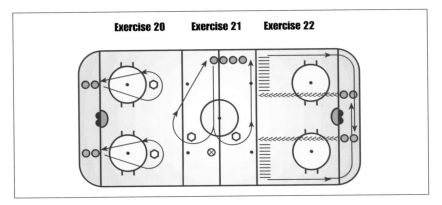

Exercise 20   **Exercise 21**   **Exercise 22**

Exercise 23

The players practice the forwards, backwards and sideways skating motions in the end area of the pitch.

Exercise 24

The players practice jumping over the sticks sideways with both legs.

Exercise 25

The players skate figures of eight using tight curves around sticks that are laid out.

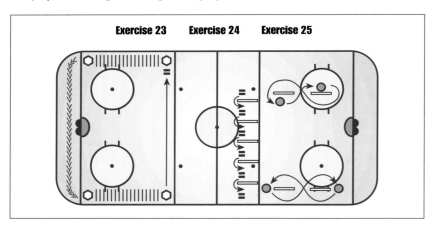

Exercise 23   Exercise 24   Exercise 25

Exercise 26

The players practice the backwards cross-over round the face-off circles, while they skate forwards in between the circles.

Exercise 27

The player skates, first of all, sideways, then does a slalom jumping hurdles and then backwards skating turning into skating forwards.

Exercise 28

The players practice the slalom round each cone using tight curves and return back skating backwards alongside the barrier rail to the start.

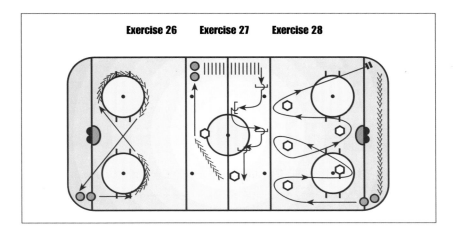

Exercise 26   Exercise 27   Exercise 28

Exercise 29

The players practice tight curves down the slalom, then do a stop and start skating off again forwards.

Exercise 30

The players practice various relay races using their ice-skating skills (tight curves round a cone, stopping, starting, turns in the curve, stopping and starting off backwards skating).

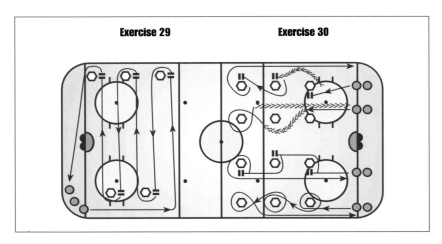

Exercise 29   Exercise 30

Exercise 31
Do a slalom using tight and wide curves alternately.

Exercise 32
Sticks are laid out on the ice in two rows not far apart. The players skate in the gap made on one leg and try to keep a straight track.

Exercise 33
The players practice skating forwards and stopping and then backwards in the other direction.

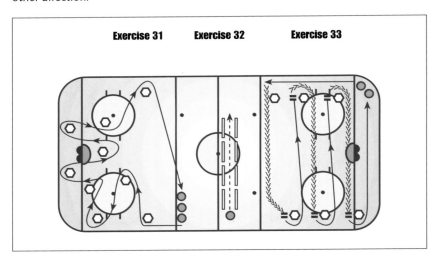

Exercise 34
The players do a figure of eight round the face-off circles, each circle is skated round 3 times.

Exercise 35
In the neutral zone, the players practice jumping over and ducking under hurdles, going sideways alongside the barrier rail, skating backwards on the blue line, and on reaching the other side, skating forwards back to the start position.

Exercise 36

The players do a slalom forwards and then behind the goal line they skate backwards again.

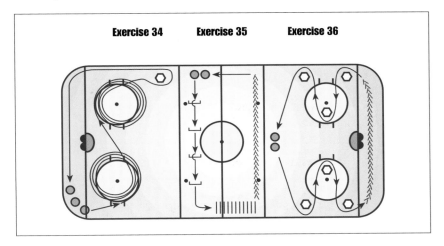

Exercise 37

The players, in two groups, skate from both corners at the same time. When they have finished the slalom they stay in the other corner of the pitch.

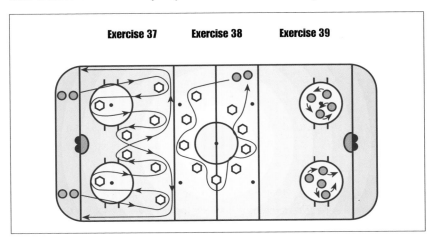

Exercise 38
The players skate the whole slalom course doing the cross-over forwards.

Exercise 39
The players move around only in the area of the face-off circles and the other players have to avoid them.

Exercise 40
Various ice-skating variations are practiced in a slalom course (cross-over forwards and backwards, skating forwards - stopping - backwards skating - stopping, tight curves around markers etc.).

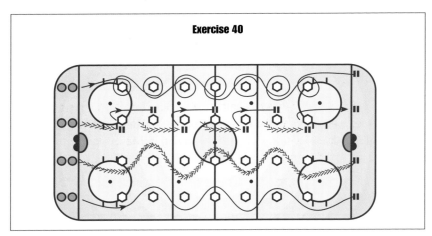

Exercise 40

Exercise 41
The players practice skating a slalom around markers erected on the face-off circles.

Exercise 42
Practice skating forwards across the pitch - turn - skate backwards - turn - skate forwards.

Exercise 43

The players skate criss-cross in the end zone of the pitch using tight curves to get round the markers and then come back along the blue line.

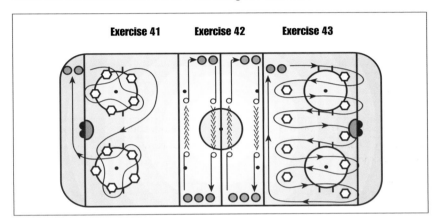

Exercise 44

On one side of the rink, the players practice a slalom round the markers using the forwards cross-over, while on the other side of the rink the players practice differing ice-skating skills (stopping, backwards skating, forwards skating with turns, tight curves around the markers).

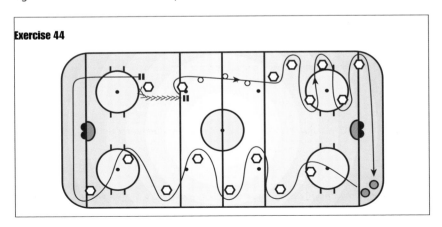

Exercise 45

The players practice the same exercises in both end zones of the pitch. They skate off from the corner, turn to skate backwards and then skate through the slalom, coming through a turn and jumping over the hurdles. Then the second half of the course is done in the same way.

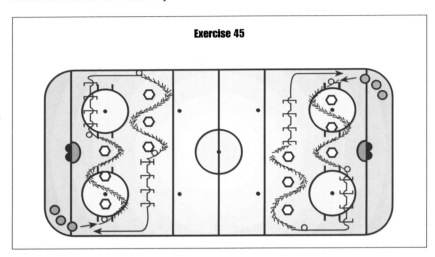

Exercise 45

SYMBOLS

⊗   Trainer

●   ●   Player

⟶   Skating forwards

⋘⋘⋘   Skating backwards

⟼   Stopping/Stop

Turn

Jump over a hurdle

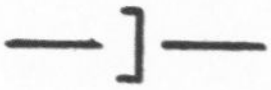

Ducking under a hurdle

⟪   Kneeling

↓   Knees bent

↑   Jump up/Jumping

∞   Switch turn

| | | | Skating sideways - this involves a special exercise for the cross-over of the legs/skating sideways crossing over the legs

⬡   Training equipment/Aids (Cones/ Markers)

▭   Ice hockey stick

PHOTO & ILLUSTRATION CREDITS

Illustrations:	Jana Tvrznikova
Diagrams:	Jens Vogelsang
Cover photo:	getty images
Inside photos:	ASA photo agency
Cover design:	Birgit Engelen

Hockey – The Basics

To renew this book take it to any of
the City Libraries before
the date due for return.